CARS

Series Creator:

David Salariya was born in Dundee, Scotland, where he studied illustration and printmaking. He has illustrated a wide range of books and has created many new series of books for publishers in the UK and overseas. In 1989 he established The Salariya Book Company. He lives in Brighton with his wife, the illustrator Shirley Willis, and their son.

Artist:

Mark Bergin was born in Hastings in 1961. He studied at Eastbourne College of Art and has specialized in historical reconstructions, aviation, and maritime subjects since 1983. He has been commissioned by aerospace companies and has illustrated a number of books on flight. He has illustrated many books in the prize-winning *Inside Story* series as well as **Space Shuttle**, **Wonders of the World**, and **Castle** in the *Fast Forward* series.

Author:

Ian Graham was born in Belfast in 1953. He studied applied physics at the City University, London, and took a postgraduate diploma in journalism at the same university, specializing in science and technology journalism. After four years as an editor of consumer electronics magazines, he became a freelance author and journalist. Since then, he has written more than one hundred non-fiction books for children and numerous magazine articles.

Editor:

Karen Barker Smith

Editorial Assistant:

Stephanie Cole

Created, designed, and produced by
THE SALARIYA BOOK COMPANY LTD
25 Marlborough Place, Brighton BN1 1UB

Repro by Modern Age.

Printed in China

ISBN 0-531-11876-2 (Lib. Bdg.)
ISBN 0-531-16442-X (Pbk.)

Published in America by Franklin Watts
Grolier Publishing Co., Inc.
Sherman Turnpike, Danbury, CT 06816

Visit Franklin Watts on the internet at:
http://publishing.grolier.com

A CIP catalog record for this book is available
from the Library of Congress.

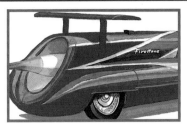

CARS

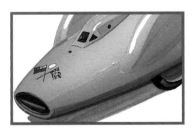

Written by
IAN GRAHAM

Illustrated by
MARK BERGIN

Created and designed by
DAVID SALARIYA

W
FRANKLIN WATTS
A Division of Grolier Publishing
NEW YORK • LONDON • HONG KONG • SYDNEY
DANBURY, CONNECTICUT

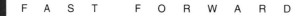

Contents

6

The First Automobiles
From the first steam carriages to
mass-produced gasoline cars.

8

The Design Revolution
From wire frames to photo-realism — using
computers to help design better cars faster.

10

Land Speed Record
The fastest driver on Earth chases the
ultimate speed record.

14

Supercars and Muscle Cars
The world's fastest, most powerful, most
desirable, and most expensive road cars.

18

Speed Kings
Formula 1 and Indy Car single-seat
track scorchers.

22

Sports Stars

"Tin top" racing with saloon cars, stock cars,
24-hour endurance racers, and rally cars.

24

Sheer Luxury

The most comfortable, elegant, and luxurious
cars in the world.

26

Car Safety

Fasten your seat belts — building safety
into cars.

30

Glossary
Car Facts

31

Chronology

32

Index

The First Automobiles

Until the 18th century, building an automobile was an impossible dream. For hundreds of years, inventors and engineers tried to think of ways of propelling a vehicle with the available technology, but they were unsuccessful. There were no engines capable of powering a vehicle until the steam engine was invented. The first steam-powered vehicle was a tractor built in 1769. Soon afterward, steam engines were built into carriages that had previously been pulled by horses, so they became known as horseless carriages. Steam carriages were noisy, slow, dirty, and often dangerous — poorly made boilers sometimes exploded! Then in 1885, the gasoline engine was invented. Because fuel was burned inside the engine, it was called an internal combustion engine. It transformed the car into a practical means of transport.

The Italian artist and scientist Leonardo da Vinci lived 300 years before the first automobiles were built. Yet among his drawings, there were several sketches of self-propelled vehicles (above).

The world's first automobile (left) was built in 1769 by a French engineer, Nicolas-Joseph Cugnot. It was a three-wheeled steam tractor that could carry four passengers at a speed of 2.2 mi (3.6 km) per hour.

Cugnot's steam tractor

Cornishman Sir Goldsworthy Gurney built a steam road-carriage (below) and began a passenger service between London and Bath with it in 1826. At first, it was fitted with mechanical legs, called propellers, to help it climb hills, but it managed without them. It performed poorly going downhill. Its brakes were too weak, and it ran out of control several times. It was also a very thirsty machine — it had to stop every 4 miles (6 kilometers) or so to re-fill its boiler with water.

The first fatal motor accident occurred on July 29, 1834, at Paisley, in Scotland, when a steam carriage designed by John Scott Russell exploded (above).

Gurney's London and Bath carriage

Most automobile engines work in four steps. Fuel and air are sucked through a valve into a cylinder (1). Then the valve closes and a piston squashes the mixture (2). A spark ignites the mixture, which expands, pushing the piston down the cylinder and turning the vehicle's wheels (3). Finally, another valve opens and the piston pushes the waste gases out (4). This is called a four-stroke cycle.

The Benz three-wheeler

Ford Model T

The first gasoline car (above) was built in 1885 by a German engineer, Karl Benz. It was a three-wheeled vehicle powered by a one-cylinder gasoline engine. The car was driven in public for the first time in the autumn of 1885, but it crashed into a wall. When Benz demonstrated it again, on July 3, 1886, it reached a top speed of 9 mph (15 kph).

American engineer Henry Ford designed the Ford Model T (above), the first car that large numbers of people could afford to buy. It was a four-seater with a four-cylinder engine and a top speed of 40 mph (65 kph). Its two-speed gears and simple springs made a drive in it rather jerky and bouncy, but its low price made it very popular. When it was first manufactured in 1908, it cost $850 (about one year's salary for a manual worker), but by 1925 its price had fallen to only $260. This made the Model T affordable to millions of people, and more than 15 million were sold by 1927, when Ford finally stopped making it.

The Volkswagen Beetle (right) is the most popular car ever built. More than 21 million of them have been sold since it went into production for the first time in 1945. The Beetle was designed in the 1930s by the Austrian engineer Ferdinand Porsche at the request of the German dictator Adolf Hitler. He asked Porsche to design a car for the people, a car that everyone could afford. The result was the Volkswagen, a German word meaning "people's car." It was later nicknamed the Beetle because its smooth and rounded body resembled the shape of a beetle.

Volkswagen Beetle

7

The Design Revolution

Every new car design begins with an idea. From there, it progresses through drawings, models, testing, prototypes, and more testing, until finally the car can go into production. The whole process of designing a new car, from the first sketch to the finished car, has been revolutionized by the use of computers and robots. Changes can be made to a design quickly with a few clicks of a mouse without having to completely re-do sets of drawings by hand. Computer simulations can check designs in a few moments without having to make models at every stage. Then, when the design is finished, robots can be programmed with the design data and can use it to produce precisely identical cars 24 hours a day.

A new car begins as an idea in a designer's head. It starts to take shape in a series of rough sketches on paper, showing the car from all angles.

Every new car design has to satisfy a number of objectives. The designer has to know if it is to be a sports car or family car, a small city car, or a roomy tourer. How many people does it have to carry? Is performance or fuel economy more important? The designer has to match these requirements, set by the manufacturer, to the car's body shape, design, materials, engineering, and international safety requirements.

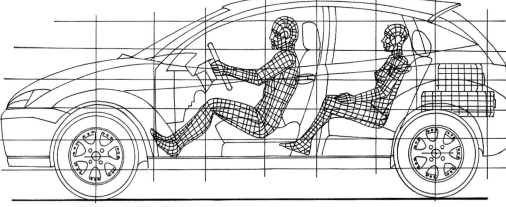

A computer-aided design (CAD) system is programmed with the shape of individual parts of the car (left). The system checks to see if it works properly and shows if there are any weak points or places where moving parts might hit each other. The CAD system enables designers to change parts of the car quickly and then check their fit and operation on the computer screen.

Information in the design computer's memory about the shape of the car is used to control a milling machine (right). This machine carves a scale model, or a full-size mock-up, of the car out of polystyrene or clay. This shows what the finished car will look like in three dimensions. The milling machine uses exactly the same data as the design computer, so the model it creates is always an accurate copy of the design car.

Computer modeling

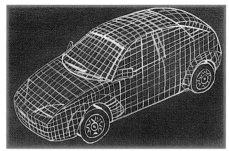

The first stage of computer modeling involves creating a wire frame image (above).

Interior details are added to the computer model to produce this X-ray view.

Adding color, texture, lighting, and shadows creates a photo-realistic image that looks like a photograph of a real car.

The shape of the car is checked by testing it in a wind tunnel (right). Small-scale models and full-size mock-ups are placed in the tunnel. Then a propeller or jet engine blows air through the tunnel. Smoke is released into the wind to show how air flows over and around the car. If the designers have done their job properly, it should flow smoothly.

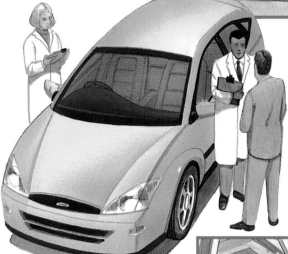

Finally, the car goes into production (right). As the chassis (the car's main frame) is moved along a production line, the steel body shell is welded onto it by robots. More robots paint the car. Then the engine is put in and the wheels fitted. The interior is put in, and, finally, the windows are sealed in place.

A few prototypes of the car are built by hand and driven on test-tracks to make sure it performs as planned. Any problems that appear are dealt with at this stage, before the car goes into production. If these precious prototypes are driven on the public roads, they are usually heavily disguised and driven only at night so that no one can see what they look like. Only a handful of motoring experts and the people who will market the new car are allowed to see it.

The car is checked, and then thousands of models are shipped to dealers and go on sale. The car is finally on the road.

9

The Land Speed Record

The greatest prize in motoring is the land speed record. Its holder is the fastest person on Earth. The current record of 763 mph (1,228 kph), set on October 15, 1997, is also the world's first supersonic land speed record.

Count Gaston de Chasseloupe-Laubat set the first land speed record of 39 mph (63 kph) in 1898.

Henry Segrave drove his *Golden Arrow* car to a record speed of 230 mph (370 kph) in 1929.

Malcolm Campbell raised the land speed record to 244 mph (393 kph) in 1931 in his Rolls-Royce powered *Bluebird* car. In 1932, he reached 252 mph (406 kph) in *Bluebird*.

In 1933, Campbell set a new record speed of 270 mph (435 kph) in *Bluebird*.

Rear wheel steering

Rolls-Royce Spey jet engines

Brake chute

Driver

Disc brakes

The current land speed record was set in a sleek black jet-powered car called *Thrust SSC*. It was specially designed and built for the job. SSC stands for *supersonic car. Thrust SSC* was powered by two Rolls-Royce Spey jet engines that are normally used in fighter planes. It was as powerful as 1,000 family cars or 140 Formula 1 racing cars. The driver, Royal Air Force fighter pilot Andy Green, sat in a cramped cockpit positioned between the two mighty jet engines. He steered by turning the two rear wheels inside the car's slender tail.

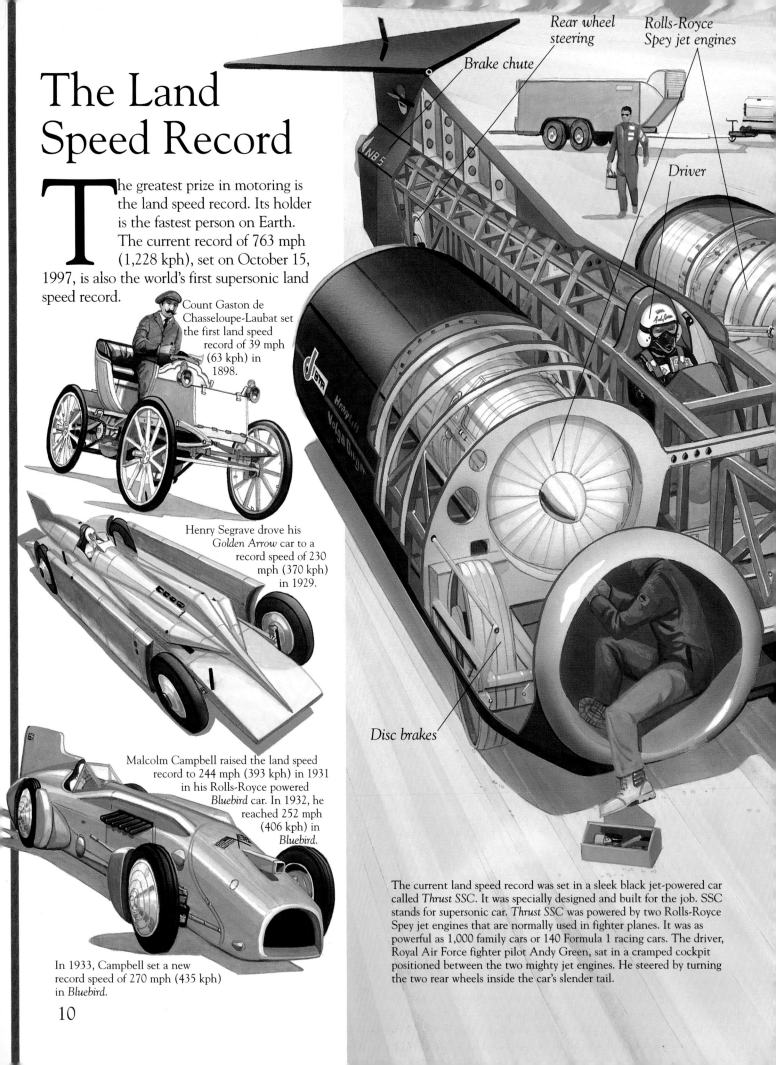

Fireman

Welded T45 steel space frame

Body shell made from aluminum, carbon fiber and titanium

Supercat all-terrain vehicle

11

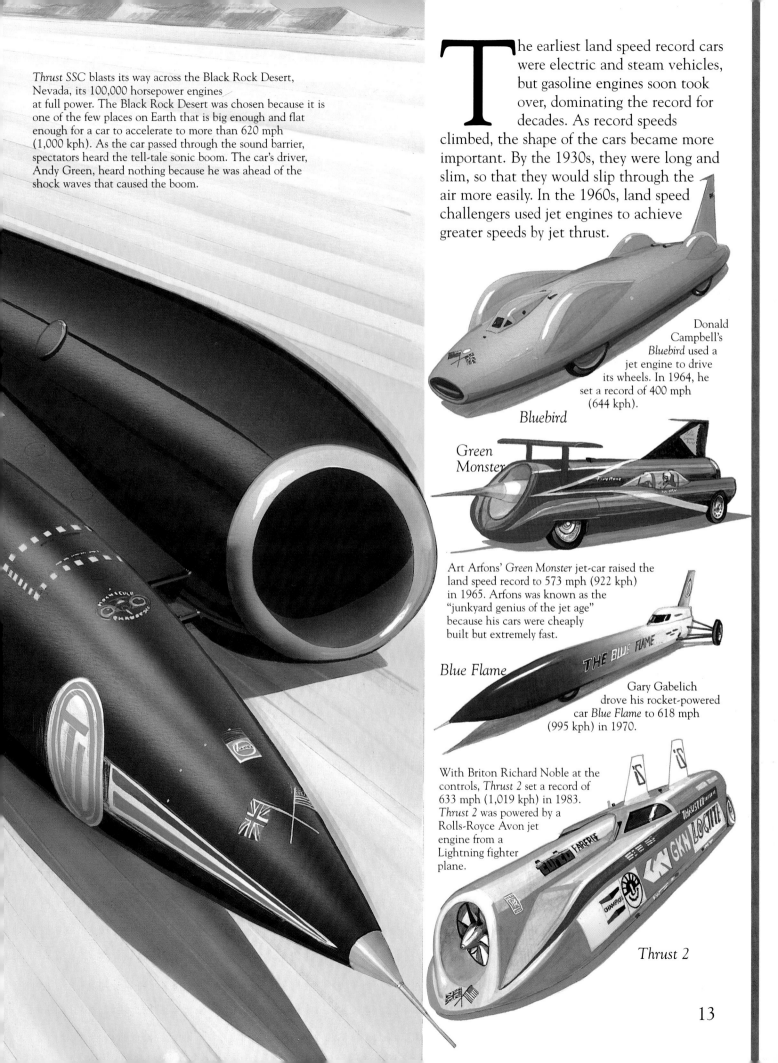

Thrust SSC blasts its way across the Black Rock Desert, Nevada, its 100,000 horsepower engines at full power. The Black Rock Desert was chosen because it is one of the few places on Earth that is big enough and flat enough for a car to accelerate to more than 620 mph (1,000 kph). As the car passed through the sound barrier, spectators heard the tell-tale sonic boom. The car's driver, Andy Green, heard nothing because he was ahead of the shock waves that caused the boom.

The earliest land speed record cars were electric and steam vehicles, but gasoline engines soon took over, dominating the record for decades. As record speeds climbed, the shape of the cars became more important. By the 1930s, they were long and slim, so that they would slip through the air more easily. In the 1960s, land speed challengers used jet engines to achieve greater speeds by jet thrust.

Donald Campbell's *Bluebird* used a jet engine to drive its wheels. In 1964, he set a record of 400 mph (644 kph).

Bluebird

Green Monster

Art Arfons' *Green Monster* jet-car raised the land speed record to 573 mph (922 kph) in 1965. Arfons was known as the "junkyard genius of the jet age" because his cars were cheaply built but extremely fast.

Blue Flame

Gary Gabelich drove his rocket-powered car *Blue Flame* to 618 mph (995 kph) in 1970.

With Briton Richard Noble at the controls, *Thrust 2* set a record of 633 mph (1,019 kph) in 1983. *Thrust 2* was powered by a Rolls-Royce Avon jet engine from a Lightning fighter plane.

Thrust 2

13

Supercars and Muscle Cars

The world's fastest road cars are the supercars and muscle cars. The ultimate supercar is the McLaren F1. It is the most powerful production car ever made and the world's first production car made from carbon fiber. Its 6.1-liter, 12-cylinder engine can rocket it to 59 mph (95 kph) in only three seconds and to a top speed of 230 mph (370 kph).

Dodge Viper

The Dodge Viper (above) is one of the most desirable American muscle cars. Its massive 8-liter, 10-cylinder engine gives the Viper a top speed of 155 mph (250 kph).

Lamborghini Diablo VT

Lamborghini's Diablo VT (above) is a beautiful Italian supercar with a 5.7-liter, 12-cylinder engine, giving it a top speed of more than 200 mph (320 kph).

The British Jaguar XJ220 (below) is even faster. Its 3.5-liter, 6-cylinder engine enables it to reach a scorching 217 mph (350 kph).

Jaguar XJ220

McLaren F1

Luggage locker

6.1-liter 12-cylinder engine

Carbon-fiber body

Water-based paint

Central driver's seat

Rising doors

Metal-coated electrically heated windshield

The Chevrolet Corvette (above) has been popular since 1953, making it America's longest lived muscle car.

While supercars are nimble and super-fast, muscle cars pack the maximum engine power. The Dodge Viper, for example, has a 450 horsepower engine under its hood, which is about five times as powerful as a typical small European city car. Because of this, muscle cars are not quiet cars — their engines have a distinctive loud roar.

The Italian car maker Ferrari is renowned for building supercars that are both elegant and extremely fast. The F50 (above) is almost a Formula 1 car for the road. Its 4.7-liter engine was modeled on Ferrari's 1990 Formula 1 racing engine. It powers the F50 to 62 mph (100 kph) in only four seconds and to a top speed of more than 155 mph (250 kph).

With a price tag of $1.5 million, the Mercedes-Benz CLK-GTR (below) is the world's most expensive road car. Its mighty 612 horsepower, 6.9-liter, 12-cylinder engine sits immediately behind the driver. When it roars into action, it boosts the 3,307 lb (1,500 kg) car to 62 mph (100 kph) in just over three seconds, 124 mph (200 kph) in less than 10 seconds and on to a top speed of 200 mph (320 kph).

Disc brakes

Electronically controlled air ducts

17

Speed Kings

The kings of the world's race tracks are the single-seat racers. Of these, the international Formula 1 and American Indy Cars are the most popular. They have rear-mounted engines to cut down the size of their noses, so they can punch through the air as fast as possible. The whole car is also slung very low between the wheels. The most extreme motor sport is drag racing. The cars, called dragsters (right), are designed to reach the maximum possible speed on a straight 1,312-ft (400-m) track.

The Indy Car 500 race is the leading single-seat motor sport event in the United States. The cars are powered by 4.0-liter, rear-mounted engines that burn methanol fuel.

The fastest dragsters of all can reach more than 310 mph (500 kph). They are so fast that they have to use parachutes to help them slow down.

Indy Cars can reach speeds in excess of 186 mph (300 kph) on the banked oval circuits used in Indy racing.

Two Formula 1 cars jockey for position. The drivers brake at the last moment to try to get to the corner first. Nose and tail wings pull the cars down onto the track and help them corner faster. Their extra-wide rear tires, made from soft, sticky rubber, transfer the maximum engine power to the track without slipping.

Jordan's pit crew crowds around one of the team's Formula 1 race cars during a pit stop. They change the wheels and re-fuel the car within a few seconds. Their fire suits protect them from fuel spills.

Juan Manuel Fangio won the Formula 1 title five times between 1951and 1957.

Sterling Moss won 16 of the 66 world championship races he entered between 1951 and 1962.

Twice-champion Jim Clark won the Formula 1 title in 1963 and 1965.

Jackie Stewart won three world titles, in 1969, 1971, and 1973.

Niki Lauda won the title three times between 1975 and 1984.

Ayrton Senna was the only driver to win three world titles before the age of 32.

Alain Prost's 51 race wins brought him four world titles.

World champion in 1994 and 1995, Michael Schumacher was the leading F1 driver of the 1990s.

Sports Stars

Almost every type of vehicle is raced, from ordinary production cars to super-expensive race cars. They are sometimes called "tin tops" to distinguish them from open cockpit single-seat race cars. Most auto races are won by the first car to cross the finish line after a set number of laps. Endurance races are different — the winner is the car that covers the greatest distance in a particular time. Endurance racing tests cars and drivers — races can last up to 24 hours. It is impossible for one driver to keep going safely for such a long time, so two or three drivers take turns to drive the same car.

A Volvo S40 fends off the competition in another close-fought round of the British Touring Car Championship (left). Touring cars are very similar to ordinary road cars as very few modifications are allowed to be made to them. Under the hood, there is a standard 2-liter engine running on unleaded gasoline. The electronic gadgetry used by many other types of racing cars to speed up gear-changing and improve road-holding is not allowed.

A Porsche GT1 turns in a winning performance at the 1998 Le Mans 24-hour endurance race (below). The race is named after the town in France where it has been held since 1923. Porsches have won more Le Mans races than any other make of car. In 1998, a Porsche won for a record 16th time.

Jeff Burton and Jeff Gordon battle for the lead during the Daytona 500 auto race (left). The Daytona 500 is one of the most famous auto races in the world. It is the star event of the NASCAR (National Association for Stock Car Auto Racing) Winston Cup series. The race is held every February, at the 2.5 mi (4 km) Daytona International Speedway, at the end of a two-week-long festival of speed called "Speedweeks."

Rally cars race against the clock, not each other. Each car sets off one minute after the car before. Road rallies are held on a course with a set of control points, which the cars must reach at set times. Special stage rallies put the cars through their paces on a series of high-speed courses across various terrain, such as forest tracks. Rally drivers are assisted by their navigator, who warns the driver what lies ahead, using intercoms built into their helmets.

Driver Carlos Sainz and navigator Luis Moya push their Team Toyota Corolla to the limit whatever the conditions. Sainz and Moya are one of the most successful rally partnerships.

23

Sheer Luxury

Luxury cars offer the highest level of comfort in motoring. They glide smoothly along the road, with hardly a whisper to be heard from their engines. They are roomy inside and have ultra-comfortable seats. Almost everything that moves is electrically powered, and the interiors are furnished with the best materials — leather seats and dashboards finished in fine wood. The ultimate luxury cars are Rolls-Royces. The Silver Seraph (below) is the most technically advanced car they have built.

The Cadillac DeVille Concours (left) is a luxury car with an electronic brain. It remembers the positions of the driver's seat, the outside mirrors, and a variety of equipment settings including the car's climate control. If any of them are changed, by another driver for example, the original positions and settings can be selected again from the car's memory. The driver's seat can even give the driver a massage!

Limousines are luxury cars that usually have a glass partition between the driver and the passengers in the back of the car. They are not usually driven by the car's owner, but by a professional driver called a chauffeur. Limousines are big cars, but some of them have been made even bigger. A stretch limo is a car such as a Lincoln Continental that has been rebuilt to make it even longer than normal.

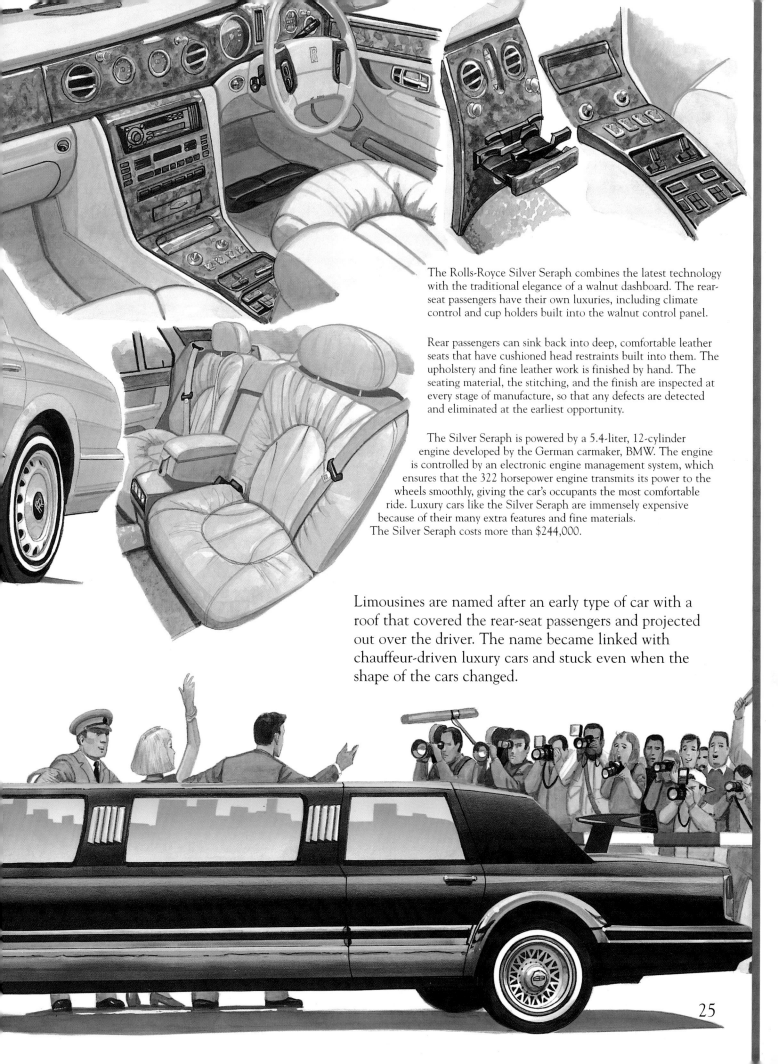

The Rolls-Royce Silver Seraph combines the latest technology with the traditional elegance of a walnut dashboard. The rear-seat passengers have their own luxuries, including climate control and cup holders built into the walnut control panel.

Rear passengers can sink back into deep, comfortable leather seats that have cushioned head restraints built into them. The upholstery and fine leather work is finished by hand. The seating material, the stitching, and the finish are inspected at every stage of manufacture, so that any defects are detected and eliminated at the earliest opportunity.

The Silver Seraph is powered by a 5.4-liter, 12-cylinder engine developed by the German carmaker, BMW. The engine is controlled by an electronic engine management system, which ensures that the 322 horsepower engine transmits its power to the wheels smoothly, giving the car's occupants the most comfortable ride. Luxury cars like the Silver Seraph are immensely expensive because of their many extra features and fine materials. The Silver Seraph costs more than $244,000.

Limousines are named after an early type of car with a roof that covered the rear-seat passengers and projected out over the driver. The name became linked with chauffeur-driven luxury cars and stuck even when the shape of the cars changed.

Car Safety

Modern cars are packed with safety devices and systems designed to protect their drivers and passengers. Before a new car is allowed to go into mass production, it has to pass a series of tests to prove that it is safe. Two different types of safety features are built into cars. Headlights, anti-lock braking systems, and eye-level brake lights help prevent accidents from happening, while seat belts, air bags, and crush zones protect the car's occupants if an accident does happen. The Swedish carmaker Volvo has been at the leading edge of car safety developments for more than 50 years.

Safety testing involves deliberately crashing some cars (above). Model drivers and passengers, called crash test dummies, are covered with instruments that record what happens to them.

Extra eye-level brake lights (right) make braking more visible to other drivers.

Grooves in the tires, called the tread (above), squeeze water out from under the tires. Without them, the car would float, out of control, on a thin film of water. This is called hydroplaning.

An anti-lock braking system (ABS) reacts when a car is about to skid. It releases and re-applies the brakes every fraction of a second, which stops the tires from losing grip.

Safety glass windshield

Alloy wheels

Deformable bumpers

Hazard flashers

Tires

The Volvo
C70 is one of
the world's safest
cars. On the outside of
the car, hazard flashers warn
other drivers if there is a problem;
deformable bumpers cause less
damage when they hit something;
and safety glass in the windshield
shatters safely, without sharp edges.

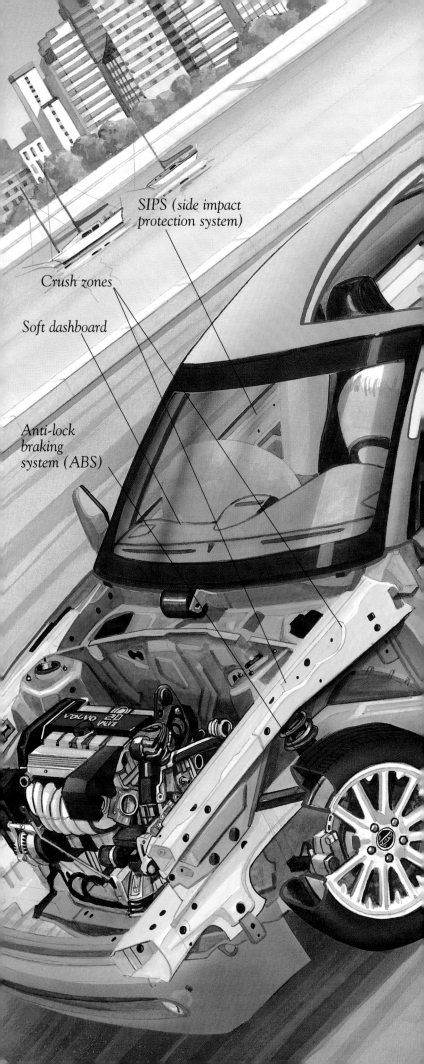

SIPS (side impact
protection system)

Crush zones

Soft dashboard

Anti-lock
braking
system (ABS)

ROPS (roll-over protection system)

Head restraints

Seat belt tensioners

Sunshade

Head restraint

Volvo's baby seat has a sunshade, a pillow to cushion the baby's head from vibration, and a head restraint for added protection from rear impacts.

WHIPS (WHIplash Protection System)

Side impact bars

Air bags

Volvo introduced air bags (right) in 1987. The bag inflates automatically during a collision and stops the driver's head from hitting the steering wheel. In 1994, Volvo introduced side impact air bags to give protection from side impacts too.

Many of the Volvo C70's safety features are hidden within the car's structure, out of sight but constantly ready for action. Most of them are designed to protect the driver and passengers from the enormous forces unleashed during a collision.

When a car is hit from behind, the driver's seat backrest accelerates forward into his or her back.

The WHIPS reduces the force of the impact by automatically moving and tilting the backrest backward.

Safety features such as crush zones work by soaking up collision energy. Volvo's WHIPS channels rear impact energy into the seat instead of the driver.

29

Glossary

Accelerate
Go faster. The pedal a driver presses to make a car go faster is called the accelerator.

Cat's eyes
Reflectors placed along some roads to reflect light from car headlights back to the drivers so that they can see the edges of traffic lanes clearly at night.

Combustion
Another word for burning.

Cylinder
A metal tube inside a car's engine where the fuel is burned. Car engines usually have four or more cylinders.

Dashboard
The panel in front of a car's driver containing all the instruments and controls.

Deformable bumper
A bumper made from a soft material that changes shape when it touches something. It is safer than a hard metal bumper in accidents involving pedestrians or cyclists.

Disc brakes
Brakes that work by using hard, rough pads to grip a steel disc fixed to each road-wheel to slow it down.

Fuel
A liquid such as gasoline or diesel that is changed to a vapor and burned inside a car engine.

Head restraint
A cushioned pad at the top of a car seat that stops the head from snapping backward and causing whiplash injuries when a car is hit from behind.

Piston
A disc that slides up and down inside an engine's cylinder.

Pit stop
A visit to the pits (garages at the side of a car racing track) by a racing car during a race to have its tires changed and/or to fill up with fuel.

Power-assisted
Operated by muscle power helped by a motor. Power-assisted steering in a car makes it easier to turn the steering wheel.

Prototype
The first, or original, model of a car used to test the car's design to make sure that everything works correctly before the car goes into production.

Valve
Part of an engine that regulates the flow of fuel and air into and out of the engine's cylinders.

Whiplash injury
An injury to the neck caused when the head moves backward quickly.

Car Facts

The fastest car in the world, *Thrust SSC*, goes faster on the ground than a jumbo jet flies through the air.

Solar cars are covered with solar cells. The cells change sunlight directly into electricity, which powers the electric motors that turn the car's wheels.

Hybrid cars have two or more engines, which they switch between automatically. An electric engine might be used for driving in town. When greater speed or acceleration is needed, the car switches to its gasoline engine.

A passenger in the back of a car that crashes at 30 mph (50 kph) is thrown forward with a force equivalent to that of a charging elephant.

Most modern cars are fitted with a catalytic converter, a device that changes some of the harmful gases in the engine's exhaust fumes into less harmful gases.

The size of a car engine is measured in liters or cubic centimeters (cc). One liter contains 1,000 cc. This is the engine's capacity — the amount of air sucked into or pushed out of the engine when the pistons move the cylinders up and down.

The clear plastic visor on the front of a car racing driver's helmet can withstand a stone hitting it at 310 mph (500 kph).

A Formula 1 racing driver can lose up to 6.5 lb (3 kg) in weight during a Grand Prix.

The Briton John Surtees is the only person to win world titles in both motorcycle racing (7 motorcycle world championships between 1956 and 1960) and Formula 1 motor racing (Formula 1 championship title in 1964).

The busiest road in the world is the San Diego Freeway in Orange County, California. It carries more than 330,000 vehicles a day.

There are about 500 million cars in use all over the world today.

Steam engines were thought to be so dangerous that a law was passed in Britain in 1865 preventing them from going faster than 4 mph (6 kph). It was called the Red Flag Act because a man carrying a red flag had to walk 180 ft (55 m) in front of the steam engines.

Chronology

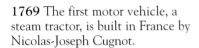

1769 The first motor vehicle, a steam tractor, is built in France by Nicolas-Joseph Cugnot.

1868 The first traffic light is set up in London. It is a gas lamp with one side red and the other green. It has to be turned by hand. It explodes, injuring the policeman who operates it.

1885 Karl Benz builds the first gasoline-driven motor car.

1887 The first motor race is organized in France, but there is only one entrant!

1891 The first electric car, called the Electrobat, is built by Morris and Salom in Philadelphia.

1893 Rudolf Diesel invents a type of internal combustion engine that is named after him.

1895 André and Edouard Michelin make the first pneumatic (air-filled) tires for cars, based on Dunlop's invention of the pneumatic tire.

1896 The first motor taxi cabs are used in Stuttgart, Germany.

1898 Count Gaston de Chasseloupe-Laubat sets the first land speed record of 39 mph (63 kph).

1899 Madame Labrousse is the first woman to take part in an auto race. She comes in fifth.

1902 Disc brakes are invented for use in military vehicles.

1905 The car bumper is invented by F. R. Simms in London.

1906 A land speed record of 121 mph (194 kph) is set by Fred Marriott in a steam car. It is the last time that a steam car is faster than a gasoline car.

1907 The world's first purpose-built motor racing circuit opens at Brooklands in Surrey, England.

1908 The Model T Ford goes into mass production in Detroit, Michigan.

1911 The first self-starter is invented for starting automobiles instead of turning a starting handle.

1914 Red and green electric traffic lights are introduced in Cleveland, Ohio.

1916 Windshield wipers are used for the first time in the United States.

1918 A third (yellow) light is added to red-green traffic lights.

1919 Hydraulic brakes (operated by oil pressure) are developed for automobiles.

1921 The first motorway is built, in Germany.

1924 Malcolm Campbell sets the first of nine land speed records, at 145 mph (233 kph).

1930 Cedric Dicksee develops a diesel engine for road vehicles.

1934 Percy Shaw invents "cat's eyes" — reflective studs that mark the edges of traffic lanes.

1935 Carlton Magee invents the parking meter in Tulsa, Oklahoma.

1947 Raymond Loewy designs the first modern streamlined car, the Studebaker.

1949 M.B. Taylor designs the Aerocar, a car that can also fly.

1950 The Formula 1 World Motor Racing Championship begins.

1951 The U.S. carmaker Chrysler fits its cars with power-assisted steering.

1953 A Jaguar car equipped with disc brakes wins the Le Mans 24-hour race, leading to the use of disc brakes in production cars.

1959 The Daytona 500 is held for the first time at the Daytona International Speedway.

1961 The five-door car, or hatch-back, is introduced by Renault.

1964 Sir Malcolm Campbell's son, Donald Campbell, sets a land speed record of 400 mph (644 kph).

1965 Craig Breedlove raises the land speed record to 597 mph (960 kph).

1968 Racing drivers begin wearing "full-face" helmets.

1970 Gary Gabelich sets a land speed record of 618 mph (995 kph) in his rocket-powered car *Blue Flame*.

1981 The air bag safety device is invented by Daimler-Benz.

1983 Richard Noble brings the land speed record back to Britain with a speed of 633 mph (1,019 kph) in his jet-car *Thrust 2*.

1994 Ayrton Senna, one of the most successful Formula 1 drivers, is killed during the San Marino Grand Prix.

1997 Andy Green sets the world's first supersonic land speed record in *Thrust SSC*. The Thrust team is led by the previous record holder, Richard Noble.

1999 Steve Cunningham sets a world land speed record for a blind person of 147 mph (237 kph) in a Dodge Viper car in England.

2000 Craig Breedlove plans to set a new land speed record in his jet-car *Spirit of America* to bring the ultimate speed record back to the United States.

Index

Illustrations are shown in **bold** type.

A
accidents 6, **6**, 26
air bags 26, **29**, 29, 31
anti-lock braking system (ABS) 26, **26**, 28
Arfons, Art 13

B
baby seat 29, **29**
Benz, Karl 7, 31
Blue Flame 13, **13**, 31
Bluebird 10, **10**, 13, **13**
BMW 25
brakes 26, 30, 31
Breedlove, Craig 31
Burton, Jeff 23

C
Cadillac DeVille Concours 24, **24**
Campbell, Donald 13, 31
Campbell, Malcolm 10, 31
car design 8-9, 30
carbon fiber 11, 14, 16
cat's eyes 30, 31
Chasseloupe-Laubat, Count Gaston de 10, **10**, 31
chauffeur 24, 25
Chevrolet Corvette **6**, 7
Clark, Jim 21, **21**
computer-aided design (CAD) 8, **8**
computer modeling 9, **9**
crash test dummies 26, **26**
crush zones 26, **28**, 29
Cugnot, Nicolas-Joseph 6, 31
cylinder 7, **7**, 30

D
dashboard 24, 25, **24**, **25**, 30
Daytona 500 race 23, **23**, 31
deformable bumpers 26, 27, 30
diesel engine 31
disc brakes 10, **17**, 31
Dodge Viper 14, **14**, 17, 31
drag racing 18
dragster 18, **18**

E
electric cars 13, 30, 31
endurance races 22

F
Fangio, Juan Manuel 21, **21**
Ferrari F50 17, **17**
Ford Model T 7, **7**, 31

Formula 1 10, 17, 18-19, **18-19**, 20, 21, **21**
Formula 1 racing 10, 17, 18-21, 31
four-stroke cycle 7
fuel 6, 7, 8, 18, 21, 30

G
Gabelich, Gary 13, 31
gasoline engine 6, 7, 13, 30
gears 7
Golden Arrow 10, **10**
Gordon, Jeff 23
Green, Andy 10, 13, 31
Green Monster 13, **13**
Gurney, Sir Goldsworthy 6

H
hatchback 31
hazard flashers **26**, 27
head restraints **29**, 30
headlights 26
horseless carriage 6
hybrid cars 30
hydroplaning 26

I
Indy Cars 18, **18**
internal combustion engine 6

J
Jaguar 31
  XJ220 14, **14**
jet engine 10, **10-11**, 13

L
Lamborghini Diablo VT 14, **14**
land speed record 10-11, 12-13, 31
Lauda, Niki 21, **21**
Le Mans 24-hour race 22, 31
Leonardo da Vinci 6
limousines 24-25, **24-25**
Lincoln Continental 24, **24-25**
luxury cars 24-25, **24-25**

M
McLaren F1 **14-15**
Mercedes-Benz CLK-GTR 17, **17**
Moss, Sterling 21, **21**
Moya, Luis 23, **23**

N
NASCAR Winston Cup 23
Noble, Richard 13, 31

P
parking meter 31

piston 7, **7**, 30
pit stop **20-21**, 21, 30
Porsche GT1 22, **22**
power-assisted steering 30, 31
Prost, Alain 21, **21**
prototypes 8, 9, **9**, 30

R
rallying 23
Red Flag Act 30
Renault 31
robots 8, 9, **9**
rocket-car 13
Roll-over protection system (ROPS) **29**
Rolls-Royce 10, 13, 24
  Silver Seraph 24-25, **24-25**
Russell, John Scott 6

S
Sainz, Carlos 23, **23**
Schumacher, Michael 21, **21**
seat belts 26
Senna, Ayrton 21, **21**, 31
Side Impact Protection System (SIPS) **28**
solar cars 30
Spey jet engines 10, **10-11**
steam cars 6, 13, 30, 31
Stewart, Jackie 21, **21**
Studebaker 31
supercars 14, **14-15**, 16, 17, **17**
Surtees, John 30

T
Thrust 2 13, **13**, 31
Thrust SSC 10, **10-11**, **12**, 13, **13**, 30, 31
tires 26, **26-27**, 30, 31
touring cars 22, **22**
Toyota Corolla 23, **23**

V
valve 7, **7**, 30
Volkswagen Beetle 7, **7**
Volvo 26
  C70 **26**, **27**, 28, 29, **29**
  S40 22, **22**

W
whiplash 29, 30
whiplash protection system (WHIPS) 29, **29**
wind tunnel 9, **9**
windshield **17**, 26, 27